Explorers to the New World

Moments in History
by Shirley Jordan

Perfection Learning®

About the Author

Shirley Jordan is a retired elementary school teacher and principal. Currently a lecturer in the teacher-training program at California State University, Fullerton, California, she sees exciting things happening in the world of social studies. Shirley loves to travel—with a preference for sites important to U.S. history.

She has had more than 50 travel articles published in recent years. It was through her travels that she became interested in "moments in history," those ironic and little-known stories that make one exclaim, "I didn't know that!" Such stories are woven throughout her books.

Art Credit: Art Today

Text © 2000 by Perfection Learning® Corporation.
All rights reserved. No part of this book may be used or reproduced in any manner whatsoever without written permission from the publisher. Printed in the United States of America. For information, contact Perfection Learning® Corporation, 1000 North Second Avenue, P.O. Box 500, Logan, Iowa 51546-0500.
Tel: 1-800-831-4190 • Fax: 1-712-644-2392
Paperback ISBN 0-7891-5125-1
Cover Craft® ISBN 0-7807-9269-6

Table of Contents

A Timeline of Important Events 4

Chapter 1. The Vikings 7

Chapter 2. Christopher Columbus: Admiral
of the Ocean Sea. 17

Chapter 3. Others Who Sailed West 26

Chapter 4. A Search for Magic Waters 28

Chapter 5. The Discoveries Continue 30

Chapter 6. Cabeza de Vaca's Long Walk 32

Chapter 7. Francisco Vásquez de Coronado 35

Chapter 8. The Secret Resting Place. 41

Chapter 9. Henry Hudson's River 46

Chapter 10. The Explorations Continue. 48

Chapter 11. Explorers to the Pacific Shores 50

Chapter 12. An Error in Navigation 54

Chapter 13. The End of an Era. 60

Glossary 61

Index. 63

A Timeline of Important Events

(Please note: Names may have various spellings.)

987 A.D. The Vikings reach North America at about this time.

1298 A.D. Marco Polo writes of his travels to the Orient.

1453 A.D. The city of Constantinople falls to the Turks. Now Europeans need a new route to China and the Indies.

1492 A.D. Christopher Columbus discovers the New World when he sails west from Spain.

1497 A.D. John Cabot, an Italian, sails under the English flag and discovers Newfoundland.

1499 A.D. Alonso de Ojeda explores the north and east coasts of South America with Amerigo Vespucci and Juan de la Cosa.

1509 A.D. Sebastian Cabot sails to the New World looking for a Northwest Passage. In later years, he explores the coastline and rivers of South America.

1510 A.D. Vasco Núñez de Balboa marches across the isthmus of Panama. He claims the Pacific Ocean, and all the land it touches, for Spain.

1513 A.D. Ponce de León, trying to reach the island of Bimini, becomes the first European to discover Florida.

1519 A.D. Hernando Cortez arrives in Mexico looking for gold. He wins Mexico for Spain on July 7, 1520.

1524 A.D. Italian Giovanni da Verrazano sails to the New World for France. He explores the Atlantic Coast from Nova Scotia to North Carolina. He is probably the first European to sail into New York's bay.

1533 A.D. In South America, Spaniard Francisco Pizarro defeats the Inca Indians of Peru.

1534 A.D. Jacques Cartier explores the St. Lawrence River, searching for a Northwest Passage.

1536 A.D. Alvar Núñez Cabeza de Vaca reaches Mexico's Pacific Coast from Florida. He and his companions have wandered for eight years.

1538 A.D. Hernando De Soto lands his exploration party in Florida with 950 men and 400 horses. He dreams of sailing down the Mississippi River.

1540 A.D. Francisco Vásquez de Coronado leads a vast army north from Mexico. They are in search of the Seven Cities of Cíbola.

1542 A.D. Portugese explorer Juan Rodríguez Cabrillo, sailing for the government of Spain, explores the coast of California. He discovers San Diego Bay.

1577 A.D. Sir Francis Drake begins a trip around the world for England.

1592 A.D. Juan de Fuca claims to have reached the present-day state of Washington. He is from Greece but sails for Spain.

1602 A.D. Sebastián Vizcaíno explores the coast of California. He recommends to his king that Spain colonize there.

1609 A.D. Henry Hudson sails up the Hudson River and claims its valley for the Dutch.

French explorer Samuel de Champlain explores most of the rivers in present-day Maine and sails south to Cape Cod.

1615 A.D. William Baffin, an Englishman, explores northeast Canada. He discovers a bay and island that are later named for him.

1634 A.D. French explorer Jean Nicolet explores the lands that are now upper Michigan and Green Bay, Wisconsin.

1682 A.D. René-Robert Cavelier de La Salle claims the Mississippi Valley and Delta for France. Later he fails in his attempt to return there.

1776 A.D. English Captain James Cook proves there is no water passage from the Pacific Ocean to Hudson Bay. He later discovers the Hawaiian Islands.

Chapter I

The Vikings

Long ago, a group of strong people lived in a cold, rugged land in northern Europe. This was nearly 500 years before Christopher Columbus came to America.

Some of these hardy, brave people lived in what is now Denmark. Other Vikings lived in the southern parts of Norway and Sweden. While most Europeans called them *Vikings,* they were also known as *Northmen* or *Norsemen.*

The Vikings were tall. Most of them had blond or red hair and blue eyes. Their skin was fair and burned easily in the sun. When the men dressed for battle, they put on helmets made of iron or leather and trimmed with gold. Then these Vikings looked even taller.

The Vikings were fishermen as well as farmers. So they lived near the seacoast. There were no gentle beaches. The coastline was rugged and broken. Wave after wave of cold, rough water crashed against the shore.

Long inlets of the sea called **fjords** reached far into the land. When a man wanted to visit his neighbor, he traveled in a small boat. It was easier than going all around the edge of the fjord by land.

Ships of all sizes were important to the Norsemen. And with the

waters so rough, those ships had to be strong. The Vikings became the best shipbuilders and sailors in the world.

A ship's **hull** was between 70 and 90 feet long. That's a bit longer than two school buses joined together. The oak vessel was about 14 feet across. It was close to 6 feet deep—about the height of a man.

Some ships had decks and some were only partly decked over. The **rudder** was a single huge oar. It was fastened to the **starboard**

side. The steersman could reach it from his place on deck.

There were two ways to power a Viking ship. A large square sail could be raised on the 40-foot mast. The sail was made of either woven wool or **linsey-woolsey**. It was often striped in bright colors like red, blue, and green.

The Vikings didn't always use a sail. When the sea was calm, or when a fjord was narrow, they took the sail down. The crew rowed the ship with long pairs of oars. Two men

were assigned to each oar. One man rowed while the other rested or did other chores about the ship.

To save space, the crewmen sat upon their sea chests when they rowed. Everything a sailor had brought on board was in that chest.

Just as important as a Viking's sailing ability was his fighting skill. And the most important things he owned were his shield, sword, and spear.

The finest shields were made of wood, metal, and leather. They were never left at home. When times were peaceful, a shield could be used as a basket to carry fish or fruit.

When Viking ships were moored in a harbor, the warriors' shields hung in an overlapping row from **bow** to **stern**. With these along the outside of the ship, the Vikings seemed even more warlike.

The Trading Years

Before 800, the Vikings were known for their trading ships. Moving from their own harbors, they would sail along the shorelines and rivers of Europe.

They offered fish, furs, whale oil, and the ivory from walrus tusks for trade. In return, these hardy men of the North took home fancy silks, dyes, and fine gold and silver jewelry.

They also took back ideas. They watched how men and women in other countries lived. Then when they returned home in spring to plant crops or in autumn to harvest them, they took their new ideas with them.

The Vikings saw others reading and writing. So they went home and made

up their own word system. The letters of their alphabet were called *runes*. There were 16 of them. Some runes looked like Roman or Greek letters.

The Vikings had no formal schools. But they educated their children well. Girls learned to run a home, swim, ride a horse, and handle weapons. Many young women also learned to read and write.

Boys were trained to be strong and heroic. As soon as he could walk, a boy learned to swim and ride, use weapons, and handle a boat. But perhaps more important, he spent a great deal of time reading the runes and writing **sagas**.

These sagas were tales of travel and brave adventures. From them, modern men and women have learned a great deal about the Vikings.

Two Kinds of Viking Ships

Around the year 800, the governments of Europe became weak. There were no strong leaders. Laws were often not followed.

About this time, some Vikings discovered they didn't have to trade. They could just take what they wanted. In fact, for a long time, some of them had been stealing instead of trading. No one came after them and punished them.

Before long, the people of northern Europe learned to watch for a special type of Viking vessel. They called it the *dragon ship.* These were swift, beautiful warships.

The bow was carved in the form of a *drekar,* or dragon. The boat's sides were low and sleek. And it turned easily.

With its low sides, everyone could see that a dragon ship

was filled with armed men. How their shields glittered in the sun!

When the people of a European village saw a dragon ship coming, they ran and hid. Their property was likely to be burned or stolen. And if they stayed, they might be killed or captured as slaves.

But some of the Vikings were honest traders. They had another kind of ship, a large, heavy vessel called a *knorr*. Its high sides provided plenty of space for the cargo to be traded.

No one was afraid when a knorr sailed into the harbor. It didn't turn easily and was too heavy to move quickly. There was no way that Vikings in a knorr could raid a village and hurry away.

So when a knorr came to a town's port, everyone with goods for sale or trade gathered at the harbor. There was entertainment and feasting. The townspeople and the Vikings had a good time together.

Leaving for New Lands

The Danish, Swedish, and Norwegian Northmen were not alike in their travels. Most of the Swedes moved east. They raided the river towns of Germany and Russia. The Danish Vikings attacked England, France, and Spain.

It was the Norwegians who would come to have an effect upon America. Sailing past England, they pushed their way into Ireland and Scotland. Later they moved on to the Faroe Islands and Iceland. These islands became part of Norway.

And how did the Vikings know these new lands lay to the west?

Tools such as the magnetic compass had not been invented yet. A captain steered by what he saw along the shore. When the ship was far out to sea, he measured the height of the sun, moon, and stars with an instrument called a **pelorus**.

But sometimes cloudy or stormy weather blotted out the sky. Then a ship might sail far off course. When the fog lasted for many days, a Viking ship would sail blindly. Sometimes it wandered into new waters and came upon undiscovered lands.

For many years, Norway had not had a strong king. Earls or chiefs who ruled small areas had governed the country. Just before the year 900, however, a powerful man named Harald Fairhair managed to gain control of much of the country. He made new laws, set new taxes, and formed a system of government.

For some Norwegians, this was a good thing. But the richest Vikings objected to this new way. Some spoke of leaving Norway.

Also, the Viking lands were becoming crowded. By law, the oldest son inherited all of his father's property. As time went on, the younger sons began to take their families and sail west. They searched for new farmlands to settle.

Erik the Red

A Viking named Erik the Red, for the color of his hair, lived in Iceland. In 982, he killed a man in a brawl. Under King Harald's new laws, some crimes were to be punished by **exile**. Murder was one of those crimes. For his punishment, Erik the Red was banished from Norwegian lands for three years.

Erik was a restless Viking. And three years was a long time.

He decided to follow the travels of another Viking named Gunbjorn. That man had accidentally found a huge new land after his ship became lost in a storm.

With some friends, Erik the Red set out in his ship. He sailed west. When the Norsemen saw the new land, they decided to stay. It was a barren and uninviting place.

But Erik and his companions chose the name *Greenland*. And as Erik hoped, other Norse families followed him there. The settlement was a success. At the end of his three-year exile, Erik the Red stayed.

This was not the end of the Viking travels. The next year, a Norseman named Bjarni Herjolfsson and his crew were blown off course on the way to Greenland. Herjolfsson and his crew spotted three new shorelines. But they did not stop to explore. All of this was entered in their log. We now know that one of those unnamed lands was North America.

Leif Eriksson

Erik the Red had a son named Leif Eriksson, or Leif the Lucky. He was as restless a Viking as his father.

Leif had read about the new lands seen by Herjolfsson. How he wanted to see them for himself!

Greenland had good stone for building. But all the wood had to be brought from Norway. Maybe he could find a new land with forests.

He went to see Herjolfsson and was able to buy his ship. He had no problem finding 35 men to go exploring with him.

Leif Eriksson was eager to leave. With little information about the lands to the west, he set out. It was the first planned attempt by a European to sail to what is now the American mainland.

The first landmark Eriksson found matched Herjolfsson's saga. There was no grass, and the soil seemed worthless. This barren spot was probably what is now called Baffin Island, Canada.

Sailing south, the crew soon sighted land again. This time the countryside was flat and wooded. White sandy beaches lined the seacoast. Here was a fine source of timber for the homes in Greenland.

Leif Eriksson gave this second discovery the name *Markland,* or forest land. Historians believe this was probably Labrador.

After just a brief stop at Markland, Leif Eriksson headed south again. Now he was searching for the last of the three strange lands sighted by Herjolfsson.

Two more days passed. Then there was a shout from the crew member on watch. Land was in sight.

The men anchored and went ashore. Here was a fine discovery indeed!

At a place where a river flowed to the sea, Leif Eriksson and his men decided to camp for the winter. They built low, snug houses from stones and grassy turf.

The river was filled with salmon. And they had a good supply of dried food. They could stay for months! They would explore this fine new land.

After the men had spent several days exploring, they began to notice a strange thing. Each day had much more daylight than Greenland or Iceland.

They recorded this in their log. And they noted that on the shortest day of the year, the sun was already up early in the morning. It did not set again until evening.

At home in Greenland, almost the whole day had been in darkness. Using this information, historians have calculated that Leif and his men were somewhere along the eastern shore of what is now America's New England states.

Leif Eriksson had found a fairer land than his father had ever explored. The water was pure. The skies were blue.

In early spring, one of the crew members ran into camp. "I have found grapes!" he cried. "They are rounder and sweeter than any our trading ships bring back." He held out his shield, piled high with the fruit. It was just one more good thing about this new land!

Leif Eriksson loaded his ship with grapes. He gathered vines from other fruits. Then he cut some timber to take back to Greenland.

Before he left, Eriksson named the new land. He called it *Vinland,* or wine land, after the grapes they'd found.

Leif Eriksson and his companions sailed from Vinland in the spring of 988. He never returned there.

But his brother Thorvald was eager to go. Following Leif's directions, he found the huts the Vikings had left in Vinland. For two summers, he and his men explored the new land.

During the second summer, Thorvald and his companions were attacked by **native** warriors. The Norsemen described these men as "paddling a boat made of skin."

Although the Vikings drove the natives away, an arrow found its mark. Thorvald fell. He was killed. He became the first European to be buried on American soil.

The crew returned to Greenland with the news of Thorvald's death. When he heard what had happened, the third son of Erik the Red, Thorstein, decided to sail to Vinland. He would bring his brother's body home.

This was not to be. After weeks of bad weather, a violent wind blew the ship back to Greenland. Soon after, Thorstein and his crew died of disease.

One Last Exploration

Viking adventurers continued to talk about the news of "Vinland the Good." How they wished there could be a permanent settlement in such a fine land.

A wealthy Norwegian named Thorfinn Karlsefni came to Greenland after Thorstein Eriksson's death. He married Thorstein's widow, Gudrid. And he had many long talks with Leif the Lucky.

In 999, Thorfinn Karlsefni agreed to lead a voyage to Vinland to start a colony. With him went 60 men, 5 women, and a large number of farm animals.

The colonists easily found Leif's huts. They settled in for a quiet winter. When spring came, they had a fearful surprise. Indian warriors, like those who had attacked before, came to the settlement.

These natives were not large, but they seemed unfriendly. Thorfinn ordered that no weapons were to be traded with them.

Before long, an Indian was killed. He was trying to steal weapons. Soon after, the natives attacked the colonists. The Vikings had to fight for their lives.

Although Thorfinn and his companions were able to fight off the natives, there seemed no hope of peace. They would have to return to Greenland.

When spring came, the Vikings packed their ship and prepared to leave Vinland. They took back vines, grapes, and animal furs.

There is no record that any Norsemen returned to Vinland's shores.

In 1492, when Christopher Columbus rediscovered America, there was still a small Viking settlement in Greenland.

Chapter 2

Christopher Columbus

Admiral of the Ocean Sea

The world is round, Christopher Columbus thought to himself. It really is round! Why do so few people understand that?

I've read the Norsemen's sagas. I've studied the journeys of my countryman, Marco Polo. Even some of the early Greeks and Egyptians thought the way I do.

If I sail west I will reach the Indies. The riches of China will fill my ships. With good winds, I could cross the ocean in ten days.

Christopher Columbus had spent his childhood watching sailors and their ships. Genoa, his Italian birthplace, was a busy port city.

Young Christopher's father was a maker of cloth. When he traveled on a boat to sell his woven goods, he sometimes took his son along. After a few years, Christopher began to travel without his father.

He visited ports on the Mediterranean Sea. And he sailed north to Ireland and even as far as the island of Iceland.

One trip in 1476 had not turned out well. The trading ship was attacked by pirates. It sank off the coast of Lisbon, Portugal.

Fighting for his life, Christopher battled the waves. Then he saw a floating oar. Desperately, he swam to it. Holding the oar, he paddled and kicked for six miles. At last, he reached the shore.

It will be hard to get back to Genoa, he thought. But Portugal is a fair land. I will stay here.

He learned to speak and read the Portuguese language. And he became a maker of charts and maps. His brother Bartholomew came to Lisbon and joined him in his business. They spent much time talking with their customers about sea journeys.

After two years, Columbus married a Portuguese woman.

They had a son named Diego.

Christopher Columbus was now 27 years old. He was happy in his adopted land.

Whenever he could, he sailed the seas. If anyone asked him to go along on a trip, he agreed. All the while, he studied the winds and the currents.

Columbus had a great dream. Someday he would sail west and reach the Indies, China, and Japan, which was then called *Cipango.*

Such a trip would take a great deal of money. He would need ships, food, and tools. A crew would have to be hired and paid. Someone powerful must be found to supply the money.

The king of Portugal would not help. He believed the best route would be east, around Africa.

The Italian leaders in Genoa also said no. They could get their riches from the Orient by overland **caravans**.

The English king was simply not interested. Rich people in many countries turned Columbus down too.

His best hope lay with King Ferdinand and Queen Isabella of

Spain. They wanted a rich new trade route that was not being used by the Portuguese.

The king and queen wanted to send Columbus across the sea. But they were fighting many wars and did not have money for exploration.

Finally, on April 17, 1492, Ferdinand and Isabella agreed. It had taken seven years of visits from Columbus. But now he would lead Spain's explorations. He would be "Admiral of the Ocean Sea."

Columbus hurried to be ready. His wife had died, so he arranged for his son to live with **monks**. And Columbus had a younger son, Ferdinand, who had a different mother. Ferdinand would stay behind with her.

In less than four months, Columbus had collected 3 ships and 120 men. Supplies filled the hold of each vessel. There were **sea biscuits**, water, wine, cheese, raisins, beans, honey, and rice. Cows were taken along for their milk and beef.

Three Brothers and a Cousin

King Ferdinand and Queen Isabella did not *buy* the ships Columbus needed. They ordered the port town of Palos to provide them. A different man owned each of the vessels. And each owner went along on the journey. These owners, however, were not in command of their ships.

The smallest ship was the *Niña,* a **caravel** with a crew of 24. The captain, Vincente Pinzón, was a fine seaman.

Martín Alonso Pinzón, brother of Vincente, was captain of another caravel, the *Pinta.* Its crew numbered 26. Among the seamen on this ship was another Pinzón brother, Diego Martín. And second in command was their cousin, Francisco.

Columbus got along well with Vincente. But he did not trust Martín Alonso. He found the man strong-willed and undependable.

The largest and finest of the three ships, the *Santa Maria,* was a **nao**. This ship was of a new design. Larger than a caravel, it had "high castle," built-up ends at the front and back. It was about 78 feet long, similar to the length of a Viking ship. Its hold was deep and carried much cargo. Some 40 men and boys crowded onto the *Santa Maria.* Columbus directed the voyage from its deck.

In those days, a ship was measured by the number of wine barrels it would hold. Each full barrel was called a "tun." Historians have figured the *Santa Maria*'s capacity at about 100 tuns.

In later years, Vincente Pinzón would return to the New World. He would discover the mouth of the Amazon River in South America.

The Journey West

On August 3, 1492, the three ships set sail from the Spanish port of Palos.

Six days later, they stopped at the Canary Islands, just west of Africa. Columbus knew the winds blew west from there.

The *Pinta*'s rudder had pulled

loose. It had to be repaired. Some sails were replaced on the *Niña*.

On September 9, they left the islands at last. Columbus was happy. Surely, the Indies lay directly to the west.

Mariners in those days had a compass. It was called a magnetic needle. Along with this, they used their own sightings of the heavens and stars. Using a tool called an ***astrolabe***, or cross staff, they matched their measurements to a printed chart to find their **latitude**.

Sailors also navigated in shallow water by *soundings*. That is, they lowered a **tallow**-covered lead weight to the seafloor to estimate depth.

After two weeks at sea, the men began to grumble. They could see nothing but endless water. The trade winds had lost their power. The ships barely moved forward at all.

Near the end of September, they had been gone six weeks. Some tropical birds flew over the ship. Sometimes a plant drifted by. Then nothing more appeared.

By early October, the men felt doomed. Would they ever see land again? Some insisted that Columbus must turn back before they all died.

But one thing kept most of the crew interested in the voyage. The king and queen had promised a reward. The first man to sight land would receive 10,000 small copper coins called **maravedis** every year for life. This would be like an extra month's salary each year for that lucky sailor.

More plants and reeds floated by. They must have come from land! The men stood eagerly on deck, searching the horizon.

Late on the night of October 11, Columbus thought he saw something in the distance. Was it a flickering light? Yes, there it was again. But it did not appear a third time.

The next morning, before dawn, a cry went up from the *Pinta*. "Land ho! Land ho!" The man who had called out was an excited

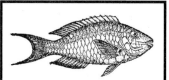

The natives of that area often fished at night, carrying burning sticks along the beach. Historians think this may be what Columbus saw from his ship.

sailor named Rodrigo de Triana. There it was on the horizon. Land! Soon everyone could see it.

But de Triana never received his reward.

Christopher Columbus insisted that his sighting of a light on shore was the first glimpse of land. The reward would go to him.

The excited explorers could hardly wait. Circling west, they found a small sheltered bay and let down several small boats.

Relieved, they fell to their knees on the beach and gave thanks to God. Admiral Christopher Columbus unrolled Spain's royal banners with their holy cross. He plunged the flagpole into the sand. Then he named the island *San Salvador,* meaning Holy Savior.

A group of nearly naked native islanders crept forward. They had never seen such men as these Spaniards. How pale their skin was. How fine their clothes. But why did they wear so many of them? The natives especially stared at Columbus. His hair had turned white when he was very young.

On this sunny beach, the Old World had come to meet the New.

The men from the three ships were lucky. The natives of San Salvador, with their painted faces and bodies, were a gentle people.

Marco Polo never wrote about such a thing, Columbus thought. But certainly these are the people of the Indies. For this reason he named them *Indians.*

Columbus soon learned just how gentle the islanders were. He wrote, "They bear no arms, nor know thereof. I showed them swords, and they grasped them by the blade and cut themselves."

The Spaniards gave the natives glass beads, mirrors, and other trinkets. Delighted, the Indians presented their visitors with parrots, woven cloth, and bits of pottery.

But it was gold that Columbus had come for. Where were the great rulers Marco Polo had met? Where were the fine palaces? Perhaps these things were on the next island.

Back on board, the Spaniards sailed south and west. One beautiful island after another appeared before their eyes. Each new island had friendly natives. The sailors tasted strange new foods. They ate sweet potatoes, kidney beans, and a grain the Indians called *maize.*

But there seemed to be no gold. No treasures.

After weeks of searching, a disappointed Columbus prepared to return to Spain. What thing of value could he take back? Ordering his men to capture a few of the natives, he prepared to sail. At least, he could show off the Indians to the king and queen.

A terrible storm came up as they were leaving. In the wind and waves, the *Pinta* became separated from the other two ships.

Columbus was furious. He had never trusted Captain Martín Alonso Pinzón or his cousin Francisco. He was sure they had sailed away to find gold for themselves.

The *Niña* and *Santa Maria* sailed about. They waited for calm seas to cross the Atlantic. On December 9, they claimed a large island, Hispaniola, for the king and queen. Today it contains two countries, Haiti and the Dominican Republic.

On December 24, the *Santa Maria* was suddenly in trouble. A careless sailor had fallen asleep on watch. Now a **reef** loomed before them.

Somehow, the ship managed to miss the reef. But a huge wave carried it onto the sand. The ship began to break up.

Jumping into the launches, the sailors rowed furiously to the *Niña.* Crowded onto that ship, they watched the *Santa Maria* sink.

Now the *Niña* was desperately overloaded. They might all drown crossing the Atlantic!

Columbus had no trouble finding 39 men willing to stay on the island. Aid came from their friends the peaceful Arawak Indians. They helped the Spaniards save most of the cargo from the wrecked *Santa Maria.* They built a fort with timbers from the ship. In it, they stored provisions, trading goods, weapons, and seedlings for planting crops.

No fort would be needed to protect them from the kindly

Arawaks. But they would need it if fierce Carib Indians came to the island.

During the first week of 1493, Columbus set sail for home. He was in a hurry. He must return to the king and queen before the *Pinta* reached Spain. Or else Martín Pinzón might take credit for his discoveries!

The return trip began peacefully. And before long, they spotted the *Pinta.* Captain Pinzón came aboard and made many excuses for his absence. Columbus wasn't sure about such stories. But he pretended to believe Pinzón. The *Niña* and *Pinta* headed for Spain.

Near the end of the trip, fierce storms blew from the north. The sea swelled and the sky grew stormy. The two caravels rolled and pitched, again and again. Through day and night, waves broke over the decks. Again, the *Pinta* disappeared from sight.

Finally, the weather grew calmer. Columbus sailed back to Spain as quickly as possible.

The *Pinta* had arrived first. But the king and queen had refused to see Martín Pinzón. Not until Columbus was with him, they said.

Furious, Pinzón went home. He crawled into his bed and refused to come out. Within a few days, he died.

Once on shore, Christopher Columbus climbed onto a burro and set out for court to see the king and queen. How proud they would be that he had reached the Indies. He took six captive Indians, a few caged parrots, and the only small sample of gold he had found on the islands.

The king and queen gave him a royal welcome. People lined the streets. He was given money and special privileges. This "Admiral of the Ocean Sea" was named governor of all the islands he had discovered.

We know now that Columbus had not found the Indies he sought. He had not discovered gold or other precious metals. But he had opened the New World to exploration.

Columbus, the finest sailor of his time, made three more

CHRISTOPHER·COLVMBVS

voyages to the New World. He either passed by, or landed on, almost all the islands in the Caribbean Sea.

But the settlements he started on those islands were often rocked by arguing and stealing. And when he returned for the men he had left in the fort, he found that everyone had been killed by a fierce tribe of Caribs from another island.

In 1504, when Columbus returned from his fourth voyage, Queen Isabella was very ill. She died before he could reach the court with his report.

King Ferdinand refused to see Columbus. Four times the king had waited for shiploads of gold from the New World. They had not come. He would not give money for more journeys. He would no longer allow Columbus to be a governor.

On May 20, 1506, in a modest house in Valladolid, Spain, Columbus died. He was 53. His servants and his two sons, Diego and Ferdinand, were at his bedside.

Christopher Columbus died insisting he had found the Orient.

Columbus proved the world was round. He discovered vast areas of North America. But, as far as historians know, he never set foot on what is now the United States.

Chapter 3

Others Who Sailed West

John Cabot, like Columbus, was an Italian. He believed he could reach the Indies by sailing west. In the 1480s, he went to England and lived in the seaport of Bristol. In 1497, he was sent by the English king to find a northerly route to China.

Cabot's travels took him to either Newfoundland or Cape Breton Island. But he never reached the shores of what is now the United States.

Sebastian Cabot sailed with his father, John Cabot, in 1497. In 1509, he made a journey of his own for England. Like his father, he also searched for a Northwest Passage to the Indies. Many historians believe he reached Hudson Bay, in what is now Canada. In later years, Cabot explored the coastline and rivers of South America.

Alonso de Ojeda was a Spanish adventurer. He sailed on Columbus's second trip to the New World. Later, from 1499 to 1500, he went on an expedition with Amerigo Vespucci and Juan de la Cosa. They explored the north and east coasts of South America. In 1505, Ojeda formed several Spanish settlements in Central America.

Amerigo Vespucci was an Italian who sailed for Spain. He went to the New World in 1499, sailing with Ojeda. He later sailed the south coast of South America for Portugal. In 1507, a German mapmaker honored him by using the name *America* on one of his charts of the New World.

Vasco Núñez de Balboa was a Spanish explorer. He first came to the New World in 1501. He settled on the island of Hispaniola. Unable to pay his debts, he ran away to Panama in 1510. Not long after, he beheaded the governor and took over Panama for himself.

Balboa was popular with the people. He led a march across Panama. When he reached the Pacific, he claimed it and all the waters it touched for Spain. Now Spaniards could see that indeed there was a New World, not just another part of India.

A Search for Magic Waters

Juan Ponce de Léon sailed on Christopher Columbus's second voyage to the New World. It was 1493 and he was 33 years old.

As a teenager, Juan had joined Spanish forces fighting the Moors of Granada. This was good experience for him. When he reached the New World, he showed he was skilled at quieting riots on the island of Hispaniola.

In 1508, the king rewarded him for his work. Ponce de León received a **commission** to explore the nearby island of Puerto Rico. He conquered that island for Spain. Then he served as its governor from 1509 to 1512.

A popular leader, he ruled the island fairly. And in 1511, he introduced sugarcane as a crop there. King Ferdinand liked the things he had done and rewarded him with riches.

But Ponce de León was restless. The natives were telling stories about a special place. It was on the island of Bimini, not far away in islands called the Bahamas.

The Indians said there was a magic spring on Bimini. If a man drank its waters, he would become young again. In 1513, King Ferdinand granted Ponce de León the right to search for this "fountain of youth."

Ponce de Léon set out with three ships to find Bimini. He had no maps to show him where the island might be. He and his men just trusted that they would find it.

On March 27, 1513, he sighted land. But it was not Bimini. It was what we now call Florida. On April 2, he landed on a warm shore near the present city of St. Augustine.

It was Easter Sunday. So he named this new place *Pascua Florida,* flowery Easter.

Ponce de León sailed all along the shores of Florida. He examined the islands of the Florida Keys and then sailed up the west coast.

There was no fountain of youth. Disappointed, he returned to Puerto Rico. Again he missed the island of Bimini along the way.

In 1514, the king gave him a royal commission to colonize the "isle of Florida." It was 1521, however, before he sailed back there. This time, two shiploads of settlers came too.

Suddenly, the Spaniards were attacked by Indians. Several settlers were killed. Another arrow found its mark too. Juan Ponce de León fell, badly wounded. He was close to death.

The settlers quickly sailed away from Florida. They sought safety on the island of Cuba. But it was too late for their leader. Ponce de León died a few days later.

Chapter

The Discoveries Continue

Hernando Cortez made several journeys from Spain to the New World. He sought new lands for his king.

Cortez tricked Mexico's Aztec Indians and their ruler, Montezuma, into trusting him. With his army's superior weapons, he and his men killed thousands of Aztecs. They won the rich country of Mexico for Spain on July 7, 1520.

Giovanni da Verrazano
was an Italian. But he was
employed by the French
government.

In 1524, he went in search
of a Northwest Passage to
Asia. Not successful in that
attempt, he explored the
Atlantic Coast from Nova
Scotia, Canada, to North
Carolina. He was probably
the first European to sail into
the bay of New York. In 1526,
he explored the West Indies
for France. While there, he
died in an Indian attack.

Jacques Cartier was a
French navigator. In
1534, he discovered the
St. Lawrence River and
claimed the area of
Quebec for France.

In his second voyage,
he revisited Quebec and
sailed up the St.
Lawrence River to what
is now Montreal. He was
not able to find a
Northwest Passage, but
his discoveries were
important. They formed
the basis for French
claims to large portions
of North America.

CLa relacion que oio Aluar nu=
ñez cabeça de vaca de lo acaefcido enlas Jndias
enla armada donde yua por gouernador p⁻
philo de narbaez/defde el año de veynt·
y fiete hafta el año ó treynta y feys
que boluio a Seuilla con tres
de fu compañia.:.

Chapter

Cabeza de Vaca's Long Walk

In 1536, a tall, tired Spaniard named Alvar Núñez Cabeza de Vaca stumbled into a small settlement on Mexico's west coast. With him were three other explorers from Spain. They were a student named Castillo, a nobleman named Dorantes, and the nobleman's black servant, Estéban.

These four were the only living members of a Spanish exploring party of 300. They had been led by Pánfilio de Narváez eight years earlier.

After landing near present-day Tampa, Florida, Narváez's men had struggled through the Everglades. Then they trudged north along the Gulf of Mexico. Disease, hunger, and angry Indians had cost them many men.

These Spaniards formed five rafts from their meager supplies. Then they sailed west along the Gulf of Mexico. They hoped to reach the Pacific Ocean.

Men continued to die of starvation. And their boats were pushed back into the gulf by the force of the Mississippi River. All but one raft was lost at sea. It was Cabeza de Vaca's that survived.

The surf tossed the raft onto an island off the coast of what is now Texas. There the men were taken prisoner by Indians. They were held for five years.

In 1534, Cabeza de Vaca, Castillo, Dorantes, and Estéban managed to escape. They set out together, walking west.

At the end of the first day, a group of kindly Indians took them in. Soon, they had food to eat and a warm place to sleep.

After several months with the Indians, Cabeza de Vaca and his three companions again began walking west. Following them were a large number of Indians who believed the Spaniards could work magic and heal the sick.

As they traveled, the Indians told the Spaniards about seven wonderful cities of gold. The cities were in a place called *Cíbola*,

in the desert lands we now know as New Mexico. Cabeza de Vaca listened carefully to the stories. But he never did see these cities.

Some of the Indians told about white men who had come earlier. They had killed the weaker Indians and taken many of the fathers away as slaves.

But what frightened the Indians most were the animals these men sat on! Terrible beasts which seemed to be a part of the men!

Cabeza de Vaca realized the natives were talking about men on horseback. Horses were a new sight to these western Indians!

After many months, the four men and their Indian followers came near the west coast of Mexico to a city called Culiacan. At a **garrison** outside of town, they were stopped by Spanish soldiers.

Instead of welcoming their fellow Spaniards, the soldiers from the garrison seized the maize the Indians were carrying for food. They announced that the Indians were now slaves.

Cabeza de Vaca and his three companions were treated like prisoners and taken farther south into Mexico. No one cared about their eight-year journey. They had heard about seven cities of gold. But they couldn't give directions to those cities. So what good were they?

In 1551, Cabeza de Vaca was sent back to Spain in the hold of a ship. He died in 1557, forgotten by the Spanish government.

But perhaps he was remembered by the American Indians of the Southwest. They had finally met a white man of honor.

Chapter

7

Francisco Vásquez de Coronado

The king of Spain was pleased. His bold *conquistadors,* or conquerors, had followed the trail set for them by Christopher Columbus and other great men of the sea. In recent years, these conquistadors had moved inland. Large Indian nations had given way to them.

In the name of Spain, Hernando Cortez had conquered the Aztecs in Mexico in 1520. Francisco Pizarro had taken over the land of the Incas in Peru in 1533.

Now it was 1535 and Spain was the most powerful nation in the world. Its lands grew until they included the Philippine Islands, most of South America, and parts of North America and Africa.

But the king had had enough of the conquistadors with their flashing swords and raiding armies. Now he needed men to govern these new lands he called "New Spain." Men who would bring peace to the people. And men who would send riches back to Spain.

King Charles sent Viceroy Mendoza to govern Mexico. With Mendoza was a young man named Francisco Vásquez de Coronado.

Coronado was from a fine family. But he was not the oldest son. According to Spanish law, the family land would not pass to him upon his father's death. So young Coronado needed a new place to settle.

Viceroy Mendoza, who may have been Coronado's uncle, kept him as his assistant in Mexico City for two years. After that, he appointed the young man governor of a large province called *Nueva Galicia,* which is now the state of Jalisco, Mexico.

Coronado settled into his new job. He would run the province the best way he could.

He was not a conquistador. He did not want to conquer anyone. He married a young woman from a fine family. It was time for Coronado to settle down.

But Viceroy Mendoza had other ideas.

Stories about Cabeza de Vaca and the Negro Estéban were sweeping Mexico. Some men said there were seven cities filled with gold!

Mendoza could not keep his mind on his duties. How proud the king would be if he, Mendoza, could find the Seven Cities of Cíbola!

But Mendoza was not a man to go exploring. He needed a leader who was brave and could handle a huge army. Someone he

could trust. Mendoza knew just the man—Francisco Coronado.

Coronado was obedient. If he was given a job to do, he would do it.

Mendoza ordered the largest exploration party ever. Coronado would lead 300 Spanish adventurers from good families. Three of them would bring their wives. With them would march several priests and 800 natives.

They would not wander about in hunger. Coronado assigned 600 pack animals to carry supplies. Servants would drive large herds of cattle and sheep. And boats would travel north up the Gulf of California to meet them with more food.

A priest, Friar Marcos, said he had once seen Cíbola from a distance. Viceroy Mendoza chose him as Coronado's guide. In April 1540, the expedition started for the lands to the north.

What a sight they were! Long blankets over the backs of the horses flowed to the ground. Each rider, his sword hanging at his side, held a lance pointed to the sky. Some of the horsemen were dressed in coats of **chain mail** to protect them from harm. Others wore metal helmets or headpieces made of tough bull hide. Colorful banners waved from long poles.

General Coronado, riding on his fine Arabian horse, led this glittering procession. The sun blazed on his gold-plated armor. A ray of light caught his huge sword of finest steel. Behind him came his personal servants with 22 well-bred horses for their leader's own use.

The cavalry followed Coronado. The infantry fell in behind them. Then came the animals and herdsmen.

Excitement ran high. No one could dream that this huge, glittering army would meet with disaster.

Coronado and his party were setting out on a trek through hundreds of miles of desert. It would

come to be called the *Jornado del Muerto,* meaning the Journey of Death.

After leaving Viceroy Mendoza at the city gates, they struggled forward for 500 miles. For 77 days, they saw nothing but desert on all sides. The terrible heat of each afternoon was replaced by bitter cold at night. Men and animals began to die in large numbers.

But on they trudged. Now water became scarce.

The boats bringing food up the Gulf of California never found them. Hunger threatened. The men began to eat the few weeds growing on the flat plains.

Nothing was the way Coronado had planned it. Where were the cities of gold? There was nothing like that here in this

barren place. Instead of jeweled settlements, they found a few tiny mud huts.

At last they came near a large, walled **pueblo**. It was a village filled with Zuni Indians. Some of the dwellings were three stories high. "There it is," cried Friar Marcos. "The City! The City! This is Cíbola!"

From a distance, the whole pueblo seemed to glisten. Bits of shiny rock called **mica** sparkled in the walls as the rays of sun caught them. But as he came closer, Coronado could see that everything was made of mud and stones.

Coronado and the other Spaniards had never planned to attack poor Indians. But by this time, hunger was driving the men nearly mad. There was food inside this village, and they must have it.

The Indians watched carefully as the explorers came near. They lined up along the walls around their city. They were ready to fight.

The Spaniards were weak from hunger. Some were ill from the long trip. But they had many more fighting men than the Indians had. And they had better weapons.

The hungry men attacked. Coronado was knocked from his horse during the fighting. But he was not badly hurt.

Quickly, his men took the Indian city. There they found just

what they needed. Food! They found beans, maize, and chicken!

There were no Seven Cities of Cíbola. There were only a few small villages made of mud. Coronado was furious with Friar Marcos and sent him back to Nueva Galicia.

Visiting some villages along the Rio Grande, Coronado found an Indian to guide them. Coronado called him *The Turk.*

This man told the Spaniards about a river to the east, six miles wide, full of fish bigger than horses. He claimed to know where gold was too. It would be found in a city to the east called *Quivira.*

In spring, the men started east. They followed The Turk. They marched all summer and into the fall. But they found nothing.

Coronado decided The Turk was leading them in circles. They would search for the Seven Cities without him.

Two days after Christmas, Francisco Coronado fell from a frisky horse. His head was badly injured, and he nearly died. His only wish was to go home to his wife in Culiacan. His searching days were over.

Coronado and his party retraced their steps to New Spain in June 1542. Only the priests were left behind. They had asked to stay and bring God's word to the Indians.

For two years, Coronado's expedition had been a failure. There were no riches. There were no Seven Cities of Cíbola.

Coronado, no longer a hero, was removed from his job as governor. He became a clerk in Mexico City. When he died there in 1554, he was 44 years old.

Although Coronado was brokenhearted not to find the Seven Cities, some important discoveries came from his travels. Three times along the lengthy journey, he stopped to send trusted men on separate explorations.

One exploring party was led by Captain Pedro de Tovar. He traveled northwest from Coronado's camp for 160 miles. There he met an ancient, wise tribe—the Hopi Indians. They told Tovar about a great river even farther west. Captain Tovar returned to tell Coronado about this great body of water. We know it today as the Colorado River.

Garcia López de Cárdenas and some of Coronado's other men went in search of this great river. When Cárdenas returned to Coronado, he reported the discovery of a huge canyon in the

ground. They had tried for three days to climb down into it. But they couldn't. It was too deep. The river far below seemed as thin as a silver thread. This was the first discovery by Europeans of the Grand Canyon in Arizona.

A third man, Hernando de Alvarado, was sent by Coronado to explore a pueblo near what is now Santa Fe, New Mexico. From there, a native led Alvarado eastward to an area almost to the Texas border. When Alvarado returned to Coronado, he reported seeing great herds of "oxen with humps on their backs." The Spaniard had, for the first time, seen the buffalo herds of the American plains.

Coronado's journey may have been a failure, for he never found what he was looking for. But we have much to remember him by.

He may have brought horses to the American West. Some historians believe that runaways from his herds became wild mustangs. These may have been ancestors to the horses the pioneers saw Indians of the western plains riding.

In his search for gold, Francisco Coronado had explored the west coast of Mexico. His men had not only discovered the Grand Canyon but had charted the path of the Rio Grande. Coronado's expedition had gone through the Texas panhandle into Oklahoma and Kansas. Because of his travels, Spain could claim a new part of the world for settlement.

Chapter

The Secret Resting Place

Hernando De Soto and his weary men stopped on the muddy bank. They looked across a river more vast than any Spaniard could imagine. The sight of the mighty Mississippi lifted their spirits.

Their struggle had been filled with hardship. Now they felt renewed.

By a route that twisted and turned, the explorers had journeyed through what is now Florida, Georgia, and South Carolina. They had touched corners of North Carolina and Tennessee. They'd zigzagged through Alabama. Then they'd walked the width of what would later be the state of Mississippi.

Other explorers in 1540 would probably have turned back. There was no gold. They had seen no sign of silver.

But Hernando De Soto was a man who wanted to know about everything around him. For months he had heard of a mighty river that lay ahead. Now he was there.

It would be dangerous to go back the way they had come. They had nearly died in the swamps. The Indians were always close to attacking. De Soto hoped the mighty river could help him.

He dreamed of building ships and sailing down the brown waters to the great gulf. From there he could sail to the island of Cuba.

De Soto had fought the Incas under Pizarro. It had made him a rich man. Rich enough to finance his own exploration of the New World. He had spent a year getting ready in Cuba. Then in 1538, he'd made his well-equipped landing in Florida. He was near what today is Tampa Bay. With him were 950 men and 400 horses.

For nearly three years, they had met one challenge after another. De Soto was not a man to turn back, and his men were loyal to his strong leadership.

How they had struggled through Florida's thick swamps! Often they were under attack from hostile Indians who wanted the Spaniards to leave. Those men from across the sea often brought sicknesses that swept through their tribes.

In Alabama, 12,000 Indians swooped down on De Soto's men. The chief was named Tuscaloosa. He had had enough of Spanish explorers.

The Spaniards wore heavy quilted jackets that were supposed to protect them from arrows. But still, De Soto lost 69 men.

Rest had come only when the expedition happened upon an occasional friendly tribe like the one led by Georgia's Queen Cofachiqui. She had given the Spaniards buckskins to protect them

from thorny brambles. She also had given them a gift of 200 pounds of pearls. This was the only treasure De Soto had found in the New World. He was brokenhearted when it was later stolen by another Indian tribe.

Now in 1540, as he stood on the riverbank, De Soto refused to rest. Almost three years of hardship lay behind him. But it was not the time to quit.

The men cleared a few acres to set up a **forge** such as a blacksmith would use. Then they set to work making rafts and barges. How they hoped they could cross the two miles of river before them!

The men finished four large rafts. They rigged them with crude sails and oars. Then, suddenly, they had visitors.

A fleet of large canoes paddled by 200 Indians appeared on the river. With them was a regal chief named Aquizo.

Aquizo stared at De Soto. But the Indian said nothing. Then he held out a gift of fish and some bundles of cakes made from crushed prunes. In a moment he was gone.

The Spaniards watched how well the Indians handled their canoes. "Clearly, the river is home to these warriors," they said.

For three more weeks, De Soto's men built barges. Some of their oldest guns had no more ammunition. So they melted those guns down to make nails.

Finally on June 18, 1541, they were ready. The explorers pushed their boats out into the whirlpools and strange currents of the Mississippi. As they set out to cross to the other side, they watched carefully for the return of Aquizo's braves.

They reached the other side without an attack. But De Soto would not rest. He pressed his men onward toward new explorations. Other Indians attacked from time to time. And as winter came near, the need for shelter became pressing. They pushed on to a settlement called *Autiamque* in what is now Arkansas. There they built a cluster of bark and log houses. The three months of winter passed in peace.

Eager to return to the great river, the men watched for signs of spring. In March as they prepared to leave Autiamque, they discovered one of the men missing. Handsome, witty Don Diego de Guzmán could not be found. De Soto sent out a search party.

A few days later, there was good news. Guzmán was alive. In fact, he had sent them a letter written on deerskin.

The others were not to worry about him. The chieftain of a nearby tribe had invited him to stay. He even offered the Spaniard his beautiful daughter in marriage. In this way, Don Diego de Guzmán, in 1542, became the first permanent European settler in what is now the United States.

De Soto's men marched southeast in hopes of finding the Mississippi once again. Now there were 1,300 of them. Some 600 friendly Indians had joined them along the way.

On they trudged. Their armor and helmets had rusted. Their spears were bent and dull.

At last they reached the Mississippi, again struggling through swampy land. All at once, De Soto broke through a tangle of vines and saw what he longed for. The rolling waters of this mighty river.

Hostile Indian lands lay before them. But word had spread about Hernando De Soto. Many chieftains believed he was a river god. They thought he would never die. This frightened the Indians, and they were afraid to attack.

Now trouble came from another source—**malaria**. The mosquitoes of the Arkansas swamp spread the disease among the weakened men. No one suspected that the sting of an insect could bring a fever. They blamed the food, the water, and the air.

Soon De Soto himself began to show signs of the illness. He burned with fever. Then he shivered with chills, even on the hottest days.

Gathering all his remaining strength, he led his men across the river again. But by then he was so weak he could neither stand nor walk. Knowing his days were numbered, he named Captain Luis Moscoso to replace him.

It was decided that the company would turn south. Perhaps they could reach the Spanish settlements in Mexico. If only the Indians along the river would not attack before they were on their way.

Hernando De Soto lost his battle with malaria. On May 21, 1542, he died. He had first spotted the Mississippi a year before.

Now there was fresh danger for his men. If the Indians had thought De Soto could not die, would they attack now that he was dead?

The Spaniards must keep the secret. As they prepared for their trip south, life at the camp continued. There was a changing of the guard. There were training exercises for the soldiers. One day, a nearby chief came to the Spanish camp and asked to see De Soto. The new leader, Moscoso, said De Soto had gone to visit his father.

The Spaniards were worried about their leader's burial. What if the Indians found De Soto's grave? One of the captains, Nuñez de Tovar, had an idea. "His memory and his glory are forever bound to this great, flowing river. Let us entrust it with the task of keeping the body of our beloved general."

The men cut down a heavy oak tree. They carved it into a massive coffin and weighted it down with rocks. De Soto's body was carefully placed inside and carried out to the deepest part of the river. With tears in their eyes, the men slid the oak coffin into the waters.

Hernando De Soto and the Mississippi River were now joined forever in a secret resting place.

Chapter

Henry Hudson's River

After the English defeated the famous Spanish Armada in 1588, Spain was no longer queen of the seas. Now Englishmen grew more and more bold. They could find a new way to reach China, Japan, and the Indies. They were sure of it. Henry Hudson was one of these Englishmen.

In 1607 and again in 1608, an English company hired Hudson to try to find a Northeast Passage to the Orient. Traveling *northeast* meant going into colder and colder waters. Hudson was stopped by ice and cold during both those expeditions.

Then, in 1609, it was a Dutch company that hired him. They, too, wanted him to go northeast. This time he sailed as far as Spitzbergen, an island between the north coast of Norway and the

North Pole. Again, he found solid ice in his way.

Hudson was furious. This is getting me nowhere, he thought. I spend weeks searching for this Northeast Passage. And each time my ship, the *Half Moon,* is stopped by the ice.

Hudson didn't go back to Holland. He didn't send a message to the Dutch company. He didn't stop to get permission. He just turned around and went the other way.

Across the Atlantic Ocean he sailed. He was disobeying orders. But the Dutch would soon forgive him. He was about to make a wonderful discovery for them.

Nearing the coast of the New World, Hudson found a handsome inlet. It was the same New York bay the Italian Verrazano had found more than 70 years before.

But Henry Hudson did not stop at the bay. He was interested in the river that stretched north. Perhaps this was the *Northwest* Passage so many men were looking for.

Hudson started up the river that now bears his name. He traveled almost all the way to the present city of Albany. And in 1609, he claimed all this land for Holland. This led to a busy Dutch fur trade in this region. A few towns began along the river.

In 1610, Hudson made another trip. This time he sailed for England and his ship was named *Discovery*. Pushing farther north than he had been before, he found Hudson Bay. This land he claimed for England.

This was a fine discovery, but it was not a passage to the Pacific. Hudson and his crew remained all through the cold, brutal winter. In spring, the crew members were hungry and sick.

Finally, the unhappy men mutinied. They forced Henry Hudson, his son, and seven loyal sailors into a boat. Then they pushed the boat away from the *Discovery* and sailed away.

Hudson and the others in the small boat were never seen again.

Chapter

The Explorations Continue

Samuel de Champlain was a French explorer. He had read about the travels of Jacques Cartier 60 years before.

Champlain traveled over much of New France, which is now Canada. He also explored most of the rivers in present-day Maine and sailed as far south as Cape Cod.

In 1609, with a party of Huron Indians, he discovered the large lake between New York and Vermont that is named for him.

William Baffin was a British explorer. He traveled through northeastern Canada. Like others, he searched for a Northwest Passage to the Orient. He explored Hudson Bay in 1615. The next year, he discovered the ice-clogged bay and the island that were both named for him.

Jean Nicolet first came to New France (eastern Canada) with Samuel de Champlain in 1618. In 1634, he became the first French explorer to pass through the Straits of Mackinac—the passage between the upper and lower peninsulas of Michigan. Nicolet explored Green Bay and the Fox River. He drowned at Trois Rivieres, a French trading post on the St. Lawrence River.

Chapter II

Explorers to the Pacific Shores

Not all the explorers to the New World came to America's eastern shore. As time went by, learned men realized that Columbus and those who came after him had found a New World. And beyond that New World lay another great ocean, the Pacific.

Juan Rodríguez Cabrillo

In 1542, Portuguese Juan Rodríguez Cabrillo explored for Spain. He was probably the first European to see the coast of what is now California.

Setting sail from Mexico, he went up North America's west coast. He was looking for riches. He also hoped to find a water passage from the Pacific Ocean to the Atlantic.

Cabrillo made a wonderful discovery—San Diego Bay in southern California. Such a deep, wide bay could protect a hundred ships from storms.

After staying there for some months, Cabrillo continued north. Although Cabrillo died of a fever while on the trip, his crew continued the voyage. Some historians believe they traveled as far north as present-day Oregon.

Sir Francis Drake

Sir Francis Drake was an English navigator and explorer. In 1577, he set out from England with five ships and 164 men. England and Spain were fighting a naval war. It was Drake's plan to raid the Spanish on the Pacific Coast of South America. This would mean riches for him. And it would weaken the Spanish fleet for the queen.

There was no Panama Canal in those days. So Drake planned to sail all the way around the south end of South America.

He lost two of his ships in the Atlantic Ocean. Another sank in a storm near the tip of South America. Still another became lost, but managed to sail back to England alone. This left Drake with but one vessel, the *Golden Hind.*

Safely rounding South America, the ship sailed north along the coast, raiding one after another of Spain's South American settlements.

But Drake could find no passage back to the Atlantic. So he continued to sail north—all the way to the present state of

Washington. Finding no river that would take him across North America, he turned his ship and sailed back to San Francisco Bay.

Drake claimed all of central California for England and named it *New Albion*. Then he crossed the Pacific, sailed around Africa, and returned to England. The whole trip had taken three years.

The *Golden Hind* was loaded with treasures! Queen Elizabeth was so pleased with what he had done that she came down to his ship. On board, she made him a *knight*. From then on, he would have the word *Sir* in front of his name.

Sir Francis Drake continued to attack Spanish ships for his queen. And he was one of the commanders of the English fleet when it defeated the Spanish Armada in 1588.

Juan de Fuca

A Greek navigator named Juan de Fuca sailed the Pacific for Spain. He claimed to have reached what is now the state of Washington in 1592. Historians are not in agreement over his claim. Some believe the first explorers to reach Washington did not arrive until 1775.

Navigational tools

Sebastián Vizcaíno

Sir Francis Drake had claimed New Albion for England. This alarmed the Spanish government. They believed California belonged to them!

Several Spanish exploring parties moved along the Pacific shore. One of these, in 1602, was led by Sebastián Vizcaíno. He named many landmarks along the coast and sent a full report to the king of Spain. In it, he recommended that Spain colonize California very soon.

Finally in 1697, the Spanish crown followed Vizcaíno's suggestion and began to establish missions in California.

Captain James Cook

Captain James Cook was the best-known explorer of the late 1700s. He came much later than many others who explored what is now the United States. But he made two important discoveries. He searched along America's northwest coast for a route to the Atlantic Ocean. He also discovered the Hawaiian Islands.

Chapter

An Error in Navigation

René-Robert Cavelier de La Salle stood proudly at the mouth of the Mississippi River. Firmly he planted the flag of France and a wooden cross in the soft, black mud. Now the vast river valley would be the property of King Louis XIV and the French people.

Little did La Salle know then, on April 9, 1682, what dangers there were. Little did he know the price he would pay for protecting that claim.

Born into a wealthy French family in 1643, La Salle was a restless young man. His father had decided that his son should become a priest. But after a while the young man did not feel such a life was for him.

When his father died suddenly, 22-year-old La Salle left the church. He wanted more exciting adventures.

According to French law, by joining a religious community, he gave up all rights to the family's fortune. So La Salle was penniless. He refused to beg for help from his relatives. He would just have to make his own way.

The eager young man sailed for Canada, then known as New France. There he claimed 40 acres for settlement and developed a prosperous fur trade.

But La Salle was still restless. He listened to the stories the Indians told. They spoke of a great river that flowed to the sea. How he longed for new discoveries!

The governor in Montreal gave La Salle permission to explore the river. But he didn't give him any money. So La Salle sold all of his Canadian land to pay for the trip.

In July 1669, 7 canoes and 24 men set out to explore the Great Lakes. They would see if a river lay to the south. Might this be a passage to the Indies?

What happened next is not clear. La Salle was not a man to take notes while he explored. But it seems clear that the men were cold and hungry. Most of them deserted him.

From time to time after that, he was seen wandering the wilderness. He appeared to be hunting, fishing, and learning the languages of the Indians.

By 1673, when La Salle had not discovered a passage to the Indies, he became discouraged. Perhaps the Mississippi did not run to the Pacific Ocean, he thought. Perhaps it flowed south to the Gulf of Mexico.

France needs a fort at the mouth of the great river, he told himself. If I could build such a fort, the king would control all of North America. No Spanish or English ship would then be able to enter or leave the great river.

Late in 1677, King Louis XIV gave La Salle permission to establish forts along the Mississippi—as many as he felt necessary. But the king said that they must all be completed within five years. Always short of money, La Salle borrowed heavily.

Building a new fort meant months of work. Often the winter weather was bitter as La Salle trudged up and down the Mississippi.

King Louis XIV

Repairs were always needed at the older forts. Men and supplies had to be replaced. And friendships with the Indians grew stronger at some times and weaker at others.

Finally on April 9, 1682, La Salle and his exploring party reached the Gulf of Mexico. There he planted his flag and cross. At last, he had claimed these lands along the great Mississippi for France.

La Salle named this great stretch of property *Louisiana,* to honor King Louis. Not since Christopher Columbus had any man claimed ownership over such a vast domain.

The trip back up the river was dangerous. Many in La Salle's party grew ill and badly weakened. All the while, they sensed the Indians were watching them.

La Salle, too, burned with fever. It was months before he was strong enough to sail for France with his report.

When he arrived home, King Louis greeted him as a hero. He

was the talk of Paris. Everyone wanted to shake his hand.

La Salle forgot his troubles with the Indians. He forgot the problems with the forts. And he forgot how sick he had been. It had all been worthwhile!

The grateful king outfitted La Salle with a fleet of four ships with full crews. About 100 soldiers would return to the New World with him. Also joining him were 30 settlers and their families. Livestock and supplies crowded the holds.

The king's orders were clear. La Salle was to build a fort and a settlement at the mouth of the Mississippi River. In the very spot where he had placed the flag and cross.

And René-Robert Cavelier de La Salle was to serve as governor over this entire Louisiana territory!

But trouble lay ahead.

Sieur de Beaujeu, a captain in the French navy, was put in charge of the four ships. Quickly, Beaujeu and La Salle discovered they were not much alike. It was going to be very hard for them to share leadership.

Beaujeu was a sailor. La Salle was an explorer who cared little

about ships. The two argued over many things. Matters grew worse daily. And La Salle again became ill with a high fever.

The French fleet neared the island of Santo Domingo. One of the ships was captured by Spanish pirates. Beaujeu was not a brave leader. So he made no effort to get it back.

Then, while La Salle lay ill on the island, there was more bad luck. Several crew members died in a barroom brawl. Others deserted their ships.

By the end of November 1684, La Salle was well enough to travel. The three remaining ships set out again. They were bound for the Gulf of Mexico.

Late in December, the men caught sight of the mainland. Beaujeu and La Salle began to argue about their location. Beaujeu feared rocks along the coast. He refused to sail close to the shore.

La Salle argued that he could not recognize the Mississippi's delta. The ship was too far from shore. How would he know where they were if he could not see the land?

The confusion and arguing continued. Their navigation was not clear. The ships drifted farther and farther west. Finally, they were 400 miles past their destination. They had reached where Corpus Christi, Texas, is today.

With great shame, La Salle admitted he was lost. Landing on a swampy shore, he and his men tried to build a fort. But they were staggering from hunger and illness. Their fort was small and weak.

The food was almost gone. There was no pure water. Diseases spread.

Indians howled during the night. They stole supplies from the settlers.

Livestock died. Rattlesnakes lurked everywhere. Two more of the ships were wrecked along the shore.

Captain Beaujeu took the one remaining ship. He said he would go back to Santo Domingo for supplies. Instead, he sailed off to France and deserted the few explorers and soldiers left on shore.

Leaving the weakest settlers at the fort, La Salle and a group of 20 men marched northeast. They hoped for a trail that would lead to Canada and help.

On the journey, the men began to fight among themselves.

They could not agree on how to divide the remaining food or the meat brought down by the hunters.

Bitter feelings took over, and three men were killed with an ax as they slept.

The murderers were frantic. They had done a terrible thing. And La Salle was a leader who would treat them harshly. They feared what he might do to them!

The guilty men planned an ambush. As La Salle walked into the campsite, they fired their pistols. With a shot through his head, René-Robert Cavelier de La Salle fell dead.

After facing many enemies, this noble explorer had finally died at the hands of his companions.

La Salle had established a great French empire in America. Sadly, he was never able to follow his king's commission to govern it.

Chapter

13

The End of an Era

The time of discovery by European powers was coming to an end. After 1700, new explorations in American territory were made by those already living in the New World.

Men like Daniel Boone, Meriwether Lewis, and William Clark opened America's new lands to settlers. They were joined by American trappers and scouts like John Charles Fremont, Kit Carson, and Jedediah Smith.

No longer would European explorers outfit their ships and sail west looking for the Orient. No longer would they find unclaimed land in the New World.

Glossary

astrolabe   instrument used to observe and figure the position of the sun, stars, moon, and planets; made before the sextant

bow   the front part of a ship

caravan   group of travelers and pack animals on a journey through deserts or unfriendly lands

caravel   a small, light ship; faster than a nao

chain mail   flexible armor made of interlocking rings

commission   authority to perform duties for someone else

exile   to banish from one's own country or home

fjord   narrow inlet between steep slopes or cliffs

forge   a furnace or shop where metal is heated and shaped

garrison   military post

hull   frame or body of a ship

latitude   measurement of distance north or south of the equator

linsey-woolsey   fabric woven with linen threads going one way and wool threads going the other. This made the fabric very strong.

malaria   disease transmitted by mosquitoes; causes high fever and chills

maravedis   small copper coins

mariner person who navigates a ship

mica a variety of shiny, colorful minerals

monk member of a religious order who lives in a monastery

nao means "ship" in Spanish. Today, we call such a ship a carrack. It was a fat, slow ship, designed for hauling cargo, not for exploring.

native belonging to a particular place by birth

pelorus navigational instrument like a mariner's compass without magnetic needles

pueblo Native American village in southwestern United States; may be several stories high

reef rocks, coral, or a ridge of sand at or near the surface of water

rudder piece of wood attached to the stern of a ship that controls turns

sagas stories written in Iceland and Norway in the 12th and 13th centuries based on history or legend

sea biscuits saltless hard biscuit, bread, or cracker; hardtack

starboard right side of a ship as one looks forward

stern the rear of a boat

tallow white solid material from the fat of cattle or sheep; used mostly in soap, candles, and lubricants

Index

Alvarado, Hernando de, 40

Baffin, William, 6, 49

Balboa, Vasco Núñez de, 4, 27

Beaujeu, Sieur de, 57–58

Bimini, 4, 29

Cabeza de Vaca, Alvar Núñez, 5, 32–34, 36

Cabrillo, Juan Rodríguez, 5, 51

Cabot
    John, 4, 26
    Sebastian, 4, 27

Canada
    Baffin Island, 13, 49
    Cape Breton Island, 26
    Hudson Bay, 6, 27, 47, 49
    Labrador, 14
    Montreal, 31, 55
    Newfoundland, 4, 26

Cape Cod, 6, 48

Cárdenas, Garcia López de, 39

Cartier, Jacques, 5, 31, 48

Champlain, Samuel de, 6, 48, 49

Columbus
    Bartholomew, 18
    Christopher, 4, 7, 16, 17–25, 26, 27, 28, 35, 50, 56

Cook, James, 6, 53

Coronado, Francisco Vásquez de, 5, 35–40

Cortez, Hernando, 5, 30, 35

Cuba, 29, 42

de Fuca, Juan, 6, 52

de la Cosa, Juan, 4, 27

De Soto, Hernando, 5, 41–45

de Triana, Rodrigo, 22

Drake, Sir Francis, 6, 51–52

Florida
    St. Augustine, 29
    Tampa, 33, 42

Erik the Red, 12–13, 15

Eriksson
    Leif, 13–15, 16
    Thorstein, 15, 16
    Thorvald, 15

Fairhair, Harald, 12

Friar Marcos, 37, 38, 39

Grand Canyon, 40

Greenland, 12, 13, 15, 16

Guzmán, Don Diego de, 43, 44

Herjolfsson, Bjarni, 13, 14

Hispaniola, 23, 27, 28

Hudson, Henry, 6, 46–47

Journey of Death, 38

Karlsefni, Thorfinn, 16

King Charles, 36

King Ferdinand, 18, 19, 21, 23, 24, 25, 29

King Louis XIV, 54, 56

La Salle, René Robert Cavelier de, 6, 54–59

Louisiana, 56, 57

Moscoso, Luis, 45

Narváez, Pánfilio de, 32–33

New Albion, 52

New World natives
    Arawaks, 23, 24
    Aztecs, 30, 35
    Caribs, 24, 25
    Chief Aquizo, 43
    Chief Tuscaloosa, 42
    Hopi, 39
    Hurons, 48
    Incas, 5, 35, 42
    Indians, 22, 23, 24, 29, 33,
        34, 38, 39, 40, 42, 43, 44,
        45, 55, 56, 57, 58
    Zunis, 38
Nicolet, Jean, 6, 49
Northeast Passage, 46
Northwest Passage, 4, 5, 27, 31,
    47, 49
Ojeda, Alonso de, 4, 27
Panama, 4, 27
Pinzón
    Diego Martín, 20
    Martín Alonso, 20, 23, 24
    Vincente, 20
Pizarro, Francisco, 5, 35, 42
Ponce de Léon, Juan, 4, 28–29
Quebec, 31
Queen Cofachiqui, 42
Queen Isabella, 18, 19, 21, 23,
    24, 25
rivers
    Colorado, 39

Mississippi, 5, 6, 33, 41, 43,
    44, 45, 54, 55, 56, 57, 58
St. Lawrence, 5, 31, 49
Rio Grande, 39, 40
San Diego Bay, 5, 51
San Salvador, 22
Santo Domingo, 58
Seven Cities of Cíbola, 5, 33,
    34, 36, 38, 39
ships
    Discovery, 47
    dragon, 10, 11
    Golden Hind, 51, 52
    Half Moon, 47
    knorr, 11
    Niña, 20, 21, 23, 24
    Pinta, 20, 21, 23, 24
    Santa Maria, 20, 23
Spanish Armada, 46, 52
Tovar
    Núñez de, 45
    Pedro de, 39
trade, 9, 10, 11, 16, 19, 21, 47,
    55
The Turk, 39
Verrazano, Giovanni da, 5, 31,
    47
Vespucci, Amerigo, 4, 27
Viceroy Mendoza, 36, 37, 38
Vikings, 4, 7–16,
Vizcaíno, Sebastían, 6, 52–53